This Book Belongs To:

_____

_____

Printed in the United States of America

ISBN 9780578428079
www.littlelearnerspublishingllc.com

Zuri & Xavi Little Learners

An Inspirational Alphabet Book

Written by Danielle Jeffrey-Elliott & Robert Elliott

Illustrated by Kaley Powers

A - is for AMAZING, just like you.
Look in the mirror. Can you see it, too?

B – is for BRILLIANT, BUBBLY and BRIGHT.
When you work hard, your future will look right.

C – is for COURAGE, which means brave, too.
Don't be afraid to be the BEST you!

TO DO:
- ☑ enter the world
- ☑ steal hearts
- ☐ learn to talk
- ☐ learn to walk

D – is for DETERMINED, the way you should be when working on great things tirelessly.

E – is for EXERCISE get up and move around, being healthy and active will keep you unwound.

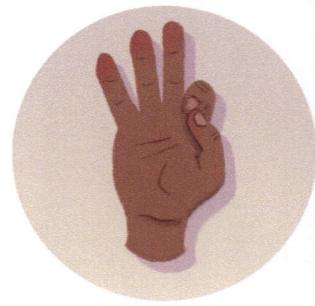

F – is for FORGIVENESS, not always easy to do, but your heart will be lighter and your troubles few.

$$E = MC^2 \qquad 2 \times 3 = 6$$
$$x = \infty \qquad 1 + 1 = 2$$
$$y = mx + b$$

G – is for GENIUS, great in one way or more. You have brains in abundance to help build and restore.

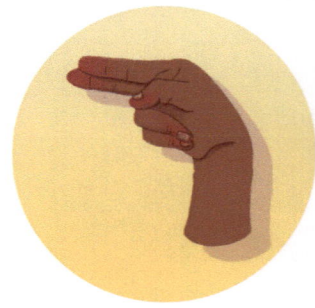

H – is for HERO, so put on your cape!
You're never too little to help save the day.

I - is for your **IMAGINATION** that's wild and free, because in this World you'll have endless possibilities.

J — is for JOVIAL, JIGGLY and JOY
all work and no play makes Jack a dull boy.

K - is for KINDNESS because it's important to share. Your kind heart and spirit with everyone, everywhere.

L – is for LOVE that you get so much of, from your parents, your friends, and the Lord up above.

M – is for MUSIC – just listen and see how some tunes and melodies can fill you with glee.

N – is for **NATURE** and **I'm** sure you know this.
Everyone should stop often to smell the roses.

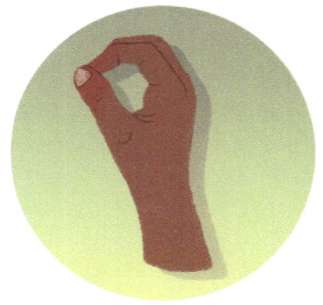

O – is for ORIGINAL, which means unique—
and that's YOU! Dream your biggest dreams and
then make them come true.

P – is for POSITIVITY, PEACE and POWER.
Three things to practice from hour to hour.

Q - is for QUEST, which is kind of a hunt.
Keep your head up, and lead from the front.

R – is for something we call RESPECT. When you show it to others—back on YOU it reflects.

S – is for SHARE, a trait that is rare. But it's also a GREAT way to show that YOU CARE.

T - is for **THOUGHTFUL**, a word that shows prudence.
Being thoughtful can grant you a world of influence.

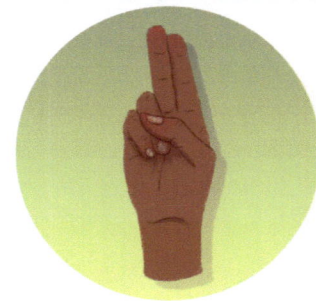

U – is for UP, the direction to head. Even on down days when you'd rather stay in bed.

V – is for **VICTORY**, finishing the race or getting the prize. And then **congratulating the others**, who also really tried.

W - is for **WINNING**, for doing something grand.
For trying, for prevailing, for taking a stand.

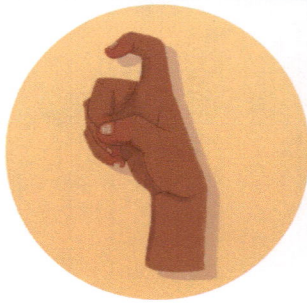

X – is for XEROX, a copy of things. But you're not a Xerox, you're as original as kings!

Y – is for YEARNING to do and be more.
Yearning can open almost any closed door.

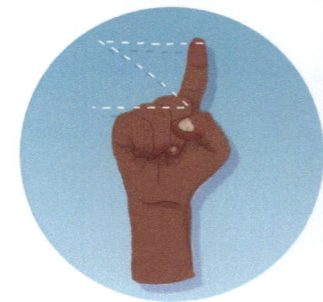

Z – is for ZEROING in on your target, we started this lesson together, but YOU sparked it.

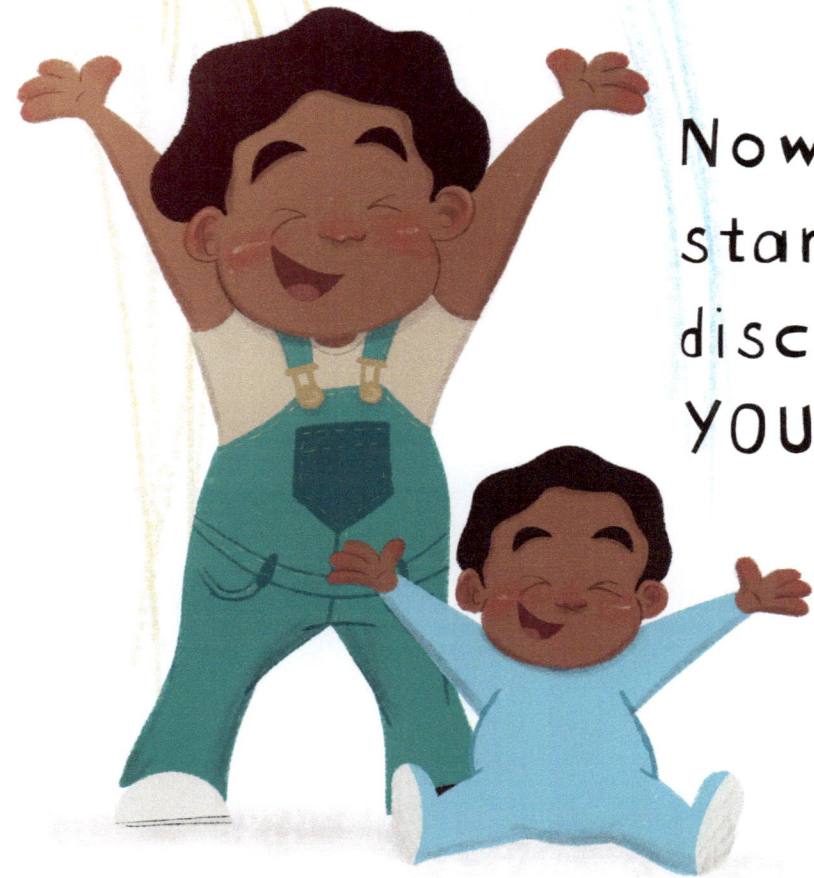

Now that you know how to start and finish, don't get discouraged: YOU'RE IN IT TO WIN IT!